MW01482998

Men Holding Eggs

MEN HOLDING EGGS

Poems by Henry Hughes

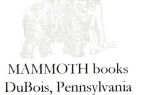

for Zoë
9-26-06
It was a great
pleasure meeting you
at U.P. Good luck
with literature + life.
warmly,

MAMMOTH books
DuBois, Pennsylvania

First Edition

ISBN: 1-59539-001-4

MAMMOTH books
is an imprint of
MAMMOTH press inc.
7 Juniata Street
DuBois, Pennsylvania 15801
www.mammothpressinc.org

Cover painting by Rebecca Marsh McCannell
Cover design by Scott McCannell
Page Layout by Mary Kay Stoddard
Author photo by Melissa Herrmann
Production by Offset Paperback Manufacturers, Inc.

for my father,
Charles Hughes

ACKNOWLEDGMENTS

Some of the poems in this manuscript first appeared in the following publications: *Antioch Review, Apostrophe, Beacon Street Review, Beloit Poetry Journal, Cape Rock, Carolina Quarterly, Clackamas Literary Review, Cream City Review, Cumberland Poetry Review, Hiram Poetry Review, Malahat Review, The North, Panhandler, Passages North, Pennsylvania English, Queen's Quarterly, Soundings East, South Dakota Review, Southern Humanities Review, Sou'wester, Tar River Poetry, Weber Studies, and Zone 3.*

Contents

IV   Away

V   Frozen Aperture

I

Men Holding Eggs

MEN HOLDING EGGS

I'm walking over the Brooklyn Bridge
with my eight-year-old sister.
I can throw her over this wall, I think.
Physical laws make it so. Easy. There are no
nets, no arms beneath the stone.

The idea sparrows through my head,
holding a Song vase at the Chait Gallery.
A thousand years of celadon blue
breaking between my black shoes.
For years I really did it—matchbox cars,
crowded jets, an HO caboose
pulled from the Christmas tracks
and tossed out a window. In the car sometimes I panicked—
made my father stop. He'd yell, I'd cry,
cry for some G.I. Joe rolling off the shoulder.

I feel it on this bridge, clasping my sister's
lemon hand. She's whistling something, her hair
bouncing light feathers
down her back. She asks about a black schooner
tacking toward the Hudson.
There are men on deck holding eggs.

THE TREE HOUSE

for my mother, Marion Spies Hughes, 1940-1978

The two of us climbed gray boards
nailed to the white oak.
We brought supplies: Devil Dogs,
two cigarettes, a Budweiser. I carried
a *Playboy* I had traded fireworks for at recess,
nervously walking through the yard,
school bag zipped tight.

Inside, October was dark.
Jays scratched
at the plywood roof.
It was cold, but the shiny pictures
kept us looking,
looking, wishing. John twisted
his cuff over the bottle's sharp cap.

I remember looking out a knothole in the wall—
the thick trees, chain-link fence,
the white-lamp curtains of the kitchen
where my mother flickered
over the counter. She gave me money
to buy *Peterson's Birds*. I spent it on a gross
of bottle rockets. I had a lot of homework,
beer on my lips.
Ten years later I bought the book,
and now, in the yard, holding its pages open,
I imagine my mother hanging
an onion bag of suet from the clothes line,
spreading grain in an old baking pan,
asking the names of birds she thought I'd know.
They are here now: fox sparrow, pine siskin, purple finch,
rusty blackbird, winter wren.
I pronounce them loudly so she can hear from the steps,
but she didn't wait for me, didn't wait to lift
these heavy words from my head.

CALLING DOWN THE GEESE

He's calling down the geese,
my uncle, low in the gray hull.
His face billows with blowing
through a wooden throat
a note all December, all bird.
He's blind. Once a savage—
beating his wife on Christmas.
I know that, watching him
listen downwind. He smiles, suddenly,
holding my arm to be still. *Be still.*
I forgive. I love this moment.
He's calling down the geese,
the gander's ear, its memory,
breath drawn across the bony dogwoods.

LEAVES OF SOUND

On the phone
we are all visionary.
Having seen only the voice
inside, we draw the secretary's perfect mouth,
a plumber's copper thumbs,
the young gardener blushing to the sound of roses
and plum.

They appear and disappear
on leaves of sound.
Age, yes. A raspy cough might crease deeply, and a tin stutter
thins the shoulders. Heavy bass,
some thickness in the waist, in the chubby hand
holding the receiver. But usually we talk smiling
for something beautiful. This can be,
always, in the electric distance
of voice.

The vertical cast
from the door. Bright hair, cheek—my eyes moving quickly,
quickly to your eyes and out
in dissolved comparison.
Here you are, standing on the steps,
hand forked like a branch, a tree
planted in sleep, watered
to die or grow
exquisitely wild.

HOLY GRAY RISING

When I last saw Todd Malcolm
he was stepping through the Pan Am gate
in tunneled fluorescence
for the Peace Corps in Zaire.
I gave him a *Field and Stream*,
said I'd send Crystal Light and Valium.
Write. What else to say? Yeah. *And if you're sick,*
get out. But for god's sake, I only wanted him to land
and gouge the lowland clay
for the carp pond he dreamt continuously
high.

I was eating cereal at dawn
when the phone rang. *Todd's dead.*
It was drizzling
but I went fishing anyway. Still *nothing*,
rereading his last letter,
nothing about the drought.
I would've signaled back to Zaire, to black men standing
on the split mud, to women
beating the dust into clouds. *The rain is coming,*
I'd yell. *Call the Pond Man back!*

Todd walked—the African lightning
too beautiful to miss, and the dazzled gazelles
flashed blue over gravel. The acacia's furrowed bark
ached, and there was one loose branch I believe
he saw and wanted for a staff. Then lightning struck
and the tree exploded
burning twenty million volts back to me,
out grounded, drifting off the bank,
drinking black New York coffee.
One pond filling, finally.
A holy gray rising between us.

After It Burns

That house with the burning cat,
and you, swinging a bucket of everything
we didn't drink. Fire foam and spray, hosing
the sidewalk so slippery
I tore my knee
and cried before a little girl. You held me,
and said, *Take it easy, only horses*
get shot for this.

Old men sifted nails and warm doorknobs
from the morning ashes. There were potatoes
baked black in the cellar
and timbers smoking like forgotten fish sticks
that cat might have loved.
I limped to the girl. *It's okay.*
There are other cats. Her mother
tightened a soggy robe
and turned her away.

Sobriety is no achievement in a dying town
with too many doorknobs. Eight o'clock
and you're the only guy who'll drink me three rooms to noon
when even the survivors collapse
in their tents, too far below the summit
to care. Last October we tried camping,
tried fires that wind inhaled.
So cold the women wanted home.
And that was the worst, you said. We promised
Hawaii in December, and still
didn't get laid.

So we're here,
and somewhere on a gravelly beach
there's a tile lighthouse and a copper cat
stroked by an old sea captain and his well-oiled
wife. The flames are white waves

cresting sharks
that go down and down in every wrinkled
wink. The lighthouse has no roof
because it doesn't need to rain. Women from our planet
hover in to worship
what should be.

ON THE WABASH

He sees gulls slice river from bank,
turning to the cracked tank where a frog grows pale
on lamplight. His brother's doing time for explosives.
Blasts along the river where a boy's
hand used to be. The Lafayette police
axeled in mud, blood
seeping through the seat they'll replace
before these boys see their father. *Aluminum don't float,*
he once said, *'less you bend it indu a boat.*

Boat-gliding over Saturdays almost cleared
the wreck of school, a house filling up with cans,
bruised smoke in the kitchen of screams. But there were rocks,
and an outboard recoiling a dead shoulder,
the anchor still in the truck, three of them drifting
with a bucket of catfish toward the *Goddamn, motherfucken bridge*
his mother wouldn't see
unless it were on TV.

Alcoa smokes across the valley
where his father might still work. There are phone calls
in the night, his mother's cough, and mornings of silence
when he draws long oars up river. Beaver burrow
yesterday's banks and the gaunt heron cocks
undreamt execution.
There's time enough in a river to bleed out
anything. And people are surprised to know
this boy catches fish and lets them go.

ICE

for Willard

On the new ice
each slide-step's a test
over something we slept through,
that rippling corner where geese huddled
gray, January lacing a feather in cold amber
you chip out for a wedding underwater
where the ice-pike hovers
like a vow.

Flying off the ax,
diamonds that would buy airplanes
for the wife you lost. *Martini shavings*, I say,
and fine cold powder behind our collars. Auger blades bite white
until that dark rush of lake. We expect to surprise the world in its still
green parlor, hunger behind the drapes, baiting
peace under cross and red flag.

But there's only waiting.
Waiting with Max one night, you say, waiting so long
for her to come home with groceries, you almost lost it.
The pale refrigerator submits to dullness. TV, empty glasses,
eyes adjusting to danger. *Some boy fell through the ice
last week*, I say. *Yeah*, you nod. *His parents
were drunks, but he was a decent kid. He loved the river.* I hear crows;
thin panes close around our lines.

Two years without affection, you say.
She had to leave. I couldn't live that way.
I drill and skim another hole,
sounding the south side, stopping suddenly
to boom and moan, some tympani the sun
turned to see. *You okay?*
Yeah, I heard it. It's okay. The crystal frequency
reporting losses.

On the ice
we know our place, our brief moment
above the world before turtles wake. Sleepy fish let us talk
and talk. A teardrop jig is an ornament and the cracks
just spaces between reason. Sure, there's some anger,
and the boy who loved water,
and your wife and son in Austin. It's a watery world,
but we are men walking on hardness,
simply because it's cold.

THE PENGUIN

In the brilliant under-light of poles,
the penguin flies through herring clouds
on unspeakable wings, her black voice draws
a thousand appetites teetering over rocks
toward a calm crystal I will never see.
Young men pull galley trays from an icebreaker
heading north. Iron music, no women,
the diesel drone loneliness
of freight.

My brother spent five years
on the Chile line and never saw a thing
but his own dick unzipped to a hundred girls
in his dreamy head. There were men, but they spoke
in onions about nothing he liked.
And when he wanted to come home
with the ten grand saved
they buried him at sea. On the ice in June she lays one egg,
warmed between her thick feet and soft down,
in the total darkness of winter.

II

Home

THE WELDER

The welder's white tongue
fuses the hull. Under a helmeted night,
stars bloom and die on the gauntlet's cuff
until the thoughtless pale returns.
He showers, salves a burn,
dresses only for the weather.
Microwave pizza, Bud Light, the TV murmuring
into sleep
where if dream were a thin match
to blow out, this storm
would kill him. Low clouds, wind off the bay.
Lightning flashes the dingy drapes
he'll never go blind to open.

Working On The Cable Team, New York, 1987

Brian shoulder-wraps black cable,
turning the wooden spool.
The two Kentuckians—Jerry and Virgil—
grab hold and dig their boots
into the soft lawn.
They all ox forward, pulling the line stiff.

In the bore pit
Darryl clears the sandy mouth of the two-inch pipe
driven under the road.
A woman brakes to watch him, waist deep,
and muscled like stone.
He yells to Brian,
Bring it in!
They feed and push,
and feed the armored wire
to me, across the road,
reaching in the dark hole.

In the yard at six
we sit on wooden spools
and drink Old Mil,
dirt drying on our arms.
Darryl says
that barmaid at the Pub Car
almost rode back to the trailer
with him. Brian's from Boston
and still talks about the Sox—
a strike away from winning the Series
then Schiraldi's pitch.
I toss an empty toward the green dumpster
and walk to my car.

At home, my father's in the kitchen,
his overalls greased, unloading his lunch box
on the counter. We eat pounds of casserole
then drink Bud on the couch, watching the Mets.
Gooden is pitching. He's my age.
My shoulders ache.

Dozing, I hear words
that might be players' names,
a signal throbbing underground.

SKYDIVING

I fell
three thousand feet,
right boot in the Great South Bay,
the left over a potato field, until the chute blew
a crippled blue, spinning,
crackling. *Christ.* I thought like a believer.
I'm really falling!
And I aimed for water,
then tore the red handle on my heart.
Sky vanished like a picnic napkin, and the round, red reserve
opened, holding me like no lover ever has.
Drifting over Long Island, there was smooth homebound
traffic, houses and stores perfectly quiet,
towers and canals shining for God.
Blown to a sod field, I bent my knees, hit,
rolled, and leapt-up
as nothing else I'd been.

DARK SPRING

The moon blind over spring tide,
Two midnight crows warm a budding ash
As rats cling and glove to hide
From cars started by a watchman's flash.
In the Island Sound bladed sharks
Clasp and copulate with rolling rounds—
Twenty minutes joining in the dark.
Few would believe in this, though some must
Have imagined truth beneath the ark.
Only I saw the boy rip the female's center
And four shark pups uncoil
In mixed blood. If I could just dive
these lights beneath the pier,
I'd drown reason, the last moon of my year.

CAPTAIN FRANK

       Captain Frank runs a party boat
to pull himself from bed.
He's too sick to dress without a reason.
His morning must be
like living under sea, truck windows
greening dimly
in dew.
I'm late to start the engine
and four stiff men
climb aboard
setting poles on the stern rail
early.

       He comes
to what's left:
the dieseled gull, diamond jigs,
and me, the mate who shows up
with one hand bandaged
and with the other pulls
bait from the well.

       At sea Frank finds a rocky ledge
where the recorder line drops
its ink. By nine he looks fine, avoiding
the sun, drinking rum
that wets his thinking. Down from the bridge,
he takes to the deck, and leans
between two men—
red-wrapped, rod tips flicking—
and tells of swordfish and sharks,
or those shadowy church parks,
late swims with hot Catholics under wine.

       Now he spots birds and bunker,
and huge bluefish aboil,
and orders me to bring her about.
But the blues disappear
when the engines growl near.
We drift blindly over oil and blood.

Softball

Chuck Harris finally found his keys
and flew across town
to Savior Field. His shoulder ached a little,
but he swung strong, singling up the middle.
He's good for forty-three, having worked out—the stretch,
morning jog, and twenty-yard sprint
from mailbox to mailbox.

The next guy hit
a little shallow, but it rolled. *Run.*
And if Chuck had not perfected his lean stride and slide—
and if the left-center fielder, twenty
with a wild arm, had not honed his aim—
this moment would have failed.

The softball
hit Chuck's temple
low in milky dust, and with a soft thud
dropped off like snow,
having stopped the joy
between that gorgeous throw
and the third baseman's unbruised mitt.

Ohio, then. Suzy Olds
in my Buick after the game, smiling, drinking beer. Chuck, Chuck.
The soft diamond barely a glimmer.
Suzy. Chuck. Chuck! *Kissing her neck. Her shirt off.*
My hand between her legs. Sirens. *Our bodies unwinding*
slowly inside the dashboard's
broken clock.

Chuck is fed by his wife,
his eyes are clear and he can walk a little. Flipping on the lights
in the garage where the bats and gloves sleep
in the trunk of his plated head—
I'll drive out of here. The fields are white,
the gates locked, but there's no time
between us. Everything is waiting. What time isn't it?
Where are the keys, the keys?

In Honor Of This Church

We were fifteen and drunk
in front of our town's first
Japanese church—the upturned sand, rolls of tarpaper,
glowing spackle buckets, a workman's shirt.
Roger pissed on the steps.
In honor of this church
I sent a silent stone arching over the lot,
heard glass hit the wooden floor inside.
Running, laughing our faces red,
my stomach splashy with beer and onion dip,
we leaped the yellow lines of Route 112,
safe in our beds at one.

There was that hazy afternoon
of old war movies—*The Sands of Iwo Jima*, John Wayne
firing into the Pacific jungles with my father
close behind on the couch. He tells me about Japs in caves,
the Death March at Bataan, and how the atom bomb
saved us a million men,
saved his brother, seventeen, on a ship outside Okinawa.

I help my father build
a shed, his beard full of sawdust,
his knees cracking as he bends for a nail.
Last night we ate salmon and talked about summer rain,
talked about wood left stacked in the yard. Through the arms
of the morning sun, I drive out to Scott Drug
for a paper, and brake early as children
cross to the Japanese Church. Small boys
in white shirts running up the lawn,
their faces like tumbled stones.
White flashing, the quickening waves
in *March of Time* news reels,
a smoky photo of my father
stiff-armed against a howitzer,
cigarette in his mouth, not knowing where
his shells are landing.

ACCIDENTAL FERRY

The back-filled bulkhead is empty
but for a cat bouncing on gold bands
of tug light. Hungover students slam
waxed car doors and wade dumbly
through a five-second horn blast. Hiking boots,
heavy denim and fleece, they rise
on deck, pointing

to the gray submarine
inside General Dynamics' watery garage.
Massive under Hollywood scaffolding
and sparks, its embryonic torpedoes
sleep unguided in the eyes of evening.

Still there's that tingle among people
going home. Even without war, even from New London
to Orient Point where you can smell destination pizza
and high school perfume in the shifting wind.
An older man smiles
as three heavy cormorants
tilt a buoy.

This ferry has done it all: landing
a thousand men and fifty tanks at Normandy.
Twenty-six trips across the channel
until it hit
another ship. What a headache
for Captain McGlew (his name's on the plaque).
But that was war.

So where do *our* accidents land us?
Car totaled on the thruway,
I ride broke and depressed
with students softly curled into sleep
on plastic benches.

Two hot dogs later, on the grease-
stained carton, I sketch
the face of a young woman sleeping

across from me. I can't draw well.
Her nose waits like a rock, her chin's a wave
cradling the mouth's silent passage.
I'm nervous. There's water all around us.
Water, all around the world.

Old Field Point, 1983

The widowed hem
of the moon, low tide, Old Field Point.
Jones and I scaling slippery rocks,
crushing crab castles, barnacle
and snail,
finding our feet to fish, to cast and hail.
Slow, he said, after so much destruction. So slow I go,
chrome-nosing that lovely lure—
a bonehead bunker—
the bluefish bites. Whitejump moonbreaks
                                and blueback runs,
till it's lost
and sung.

We smoked some *chowder*,
and thought water, thought fins and places we might be someday.
Sometimes when I'm stoned
the idea of an idea
fools me for an idea. A black kite that found a crow,
an old woman with a hoe. Write it down, write it down—
and I don't.

I wonder what kind of power or terror
real brilliance gives a person.
Wonder what I might've said to the world
at eighteen, fishing off Long Island,
pulling another beer out of my pocket
as Jones arced back into a leapingblue
                              everything
that made me forget.

THIS IS AN ANT

Do you still wake up amazed, sad
that the only world is in your head? A sparrow picks bread,
lindens breathe, and that small brown spider
has webbed the porch again. Spider? What does it matter
if you see her suck enough of Sunday's blood
to shed and lay eggs? She can't *think* you.
Hunger's in the kitchen now—coffee, toast, a leftover donut—and,

                                                        oh, ants

but from where? Think of moist places, a neighbor jogging,
then stare out the window
draped with onion skins. *Cells*, a teacher once said, scraping her cheek,
while farmer ants tunneled between glass. *Smash it*,
you thought for a second, eating macaroni & cheese.
You think of it now as they type into the house,
single notes lettered from a stuck key across the counter,
tracking a journey made small enough
to understand. Understand? Does the queen understand it's spring?
Glossy calendar guarding combs of light. Monday—nothing will happen
to change this, Tuesday—you might die
or have sex with a friend, Wednesday—you will remember
the death of a child. You always wake, piss, eat,
read something that could be heard in another voice.
Newspapers on the porch,
the *Science Times.* You look at pictures and think *this is an ant,*
but not the one walking the wall, the one you can
scoop up and throw into the web.

III

Glistening Fur

God Is A Squirrel

Radio on the picnic table,
Mom in shorts and red gloves sinking
bulbs with a forked spade.
You're dirty, I tell her. *Turn up the radio*, she says.
And bring me a beer!

On the walk,
my sneakers squish black prints you could smell.
Cat shit, she says, flicking it into the bushes,
then turning-up a cave of acorns—their pale points soft
but very certain. *God is a squirrel*, she tells me,
standing through the frequency, all crackle behind us,
the trees scratching the old windsong
of winter, and from their crowns a view of the world.

Leaves pressed in a gardener's bible,
a rusty shovel, and the dry-bagged walnut
sapling that never made it out of the garage.
Sundays always ask what we should do,
and what we should believe
when there's rustling in the attic,
when someone finally eats
those dusty nuts on the coffee table.

HOLIDAY

each evening bent like the point of a thumb tack
that will no longer stick
in

—Charles Bukowski

After
flushing the toilet
I hear drums. A Thanksgiving parade.
In my green robe I walk out to the porch
and see White Lake's high school band—
black buffalo hats, the last row out of step.
They're playing *Twist and Shout*,
and the twelve-year-old tap dancers glitter
in purple leotards, each one with an odd jacket.
Somebody's mother yells *Zip up*!
Me? My robe doesn't have a zipper. Then I think:
Shit. I got drunk with Jennifer Jordan last night.
Is that her watching from the bakery steps?
Did Jenn make it out of bed, is that the brown hair
I remember like bourbon?
The fire trucks turn onto Main, and the second pumper
wails and flashes—I'm nearly blinded, my head pounds. I'm dizzy.
But oh, the night thumps back—
rocking mattress, Jennifer
telling me to come. And I tried,
but the whole ceiling collapsed on me.
I stop whirling and throw-up
in a garbage can, go back to bed.
I'm in the middle of my holiday.

In The Doghouse

Once loved,
there's the eternal quilted hill above the floor.
No mosquitoes, no rain. Your antless dish
in the kitchen. And she strokes you,
rubs your ears. Until you slip-up—
chew the table leg, hump the wrong guest,
eat a cheesecake,
pee.

You're in the dog house,
on that rusty chain of words bolted to a stud.
There's a leafy wind, cat prints
pucker the sandy plywood floor.
You're alone. It's damp. Greasy fur pinched on a nailhead.
Sniff the corner, turn
and drop. You're not sorry,
you do your time.

Glistening Fur

Council Bluffs, Iowa

The pool table was theirs
for three hours. Hard mouths—
Fucker, Douchebag. And the huge one
backed into me and spat. Then we had them—
one easy ball to win.
But you leaned to shoot
and lost it—
a seizure that scared the town
until I sprawled to hold you down.

A couple days later in the backyard
you tell me doctors are assholes—
Don't know shit. I listen, pet the dog,
Paul, I say, *your face is a wreck.* Scratch an old scab
and the woods scratch back—
possums up from root burrows,
in leaves, in dead heels,
cracking beetles and brown eggs.
The dog barks and runs.

Where you going? Hey. I call 'round the house,
and hear a snarl,
crashing in the garbage cans—
something trying to hold on.
You flip the floods
and light the circle of trash
and glistening fur.

I know possums can stay alive
by dying.
But this one tears the dog's head
down. *Jesus, man. Look at that thing!*
You grab a board
and wedge
into blood and raw ears. The dog's cry

is fire—its eye half out.
And in this glow you're beautiful—
muscles drawn from neck to bare shoulder,
arms cut to separate peace.

CRANE MOON

Five o'clock,
corn twisted like iron,
dry glazed oaks,
the sandhill cranes filling the fields
of northwest Indiana.
Beneath the broken clouds,
the washed lines of reddening light,
a pair leafs out
broadwinged against the sun
with long hollow bones, the upward flick
of a feathered wrist.

Rust-stained,
they pick at the earth,
and dance,
bowing low and leaping
open-sailed
throwing leaves over their red crowns
bouncing like loose planets
beside the bleached grass.

It's dark now
under the crane moon.
There's nothing on the road to Indianapolis.
And nothing in the car,
but a blue robe in a suitcase
and magazines full of shining animals.

GAR

Gar unguarded
low inside Indiana's
two o'clock heat
strikes
the plastic lure and lets go—
not believing the world
has turned so hard.

It has.
And there are no limits to art.
So hand me that arrow
and take the paddle.
There, toward the teeth,
the shad-long
red
swallow.

But seeing it eat again
and again
for its own ancient self
makes my heart
so terribly full of gar,
the underworld
insatiability of it all.

Bow drawn
behind the steel point
its simple head
won't know from lightning
as we devolve
in the Eveless garden
without hunger
or knowledge.
Who needs to know the past
when we can see the gar
and kill it?

The Eyes Behind Ignite

The boss broke his tooth
in a bagel
and we got the afternoon off.
Kissed in the parking lot, ate McDonald's,
and drove the city's lungs
at stereo-speed.
Orange tunnel lights
tigered our faces

and the second cold beer
inspired grace
over a shadeless field where a crazed goat
lost his feet.
Did you see that?
Yeah. I pulled over and cradled
the blind billy onto the back seat.
A farmer's tin chimney
yammered praise.

Air-conditioning, U2, the Plymouth
ascends the mountain slope.
There's the last house, the last cool creek
before the blazing rock,
but we're not stopping.
A line from God
threads our destiny.
Then the eyes behind
ignite.

THE FOX

Out the garage door,
out to the trapline path
where I met Tony in his bait-
stained parka. We walked
a quarter-mile wood
into the papered field behind Island Bank
to catch possums, an occasional coon.
This morning only a rabbit
curled hard around a waxed spring.
Tony never said *dead*, only *finished*,
or *frozen stiff*.
I didn't want to tell him.
An hour ago Aunt Lil burned eggs to the pan,
my father drank coffee
with the policeman.
My mother died in the night and I was the only one
dressed for December.

On slow days Tony would say
this is where she was,
remembering the shock of red, black legs pulling
chain from the snow mound where we
buried a dove. A year ago, our only fox.
One crack to the brain.
Leaky-pink teeth, steam, urine. The tail
brushing against my neck
as I carried it home.
Jesus, it's beautiful, my father said.
But my mother went wild
screaming into the garage where it hung.

She never stopped. Hysterical, suddenly before dinner,
stroking my head, telling me to promise
for the fox, the brilliant fox.
Dad said *no trapping this winter*.
But we went out, Tony and I, every morning,
this morning, looking for the pointed tracks,

planting birds to lure back
that soft hair,
those thin-faced nerves
across the exhausting highway.

Music For The Shark

I walk up from the beach
where the blazing sun has driven everything
into water or sky,
and hear my sister playing piano.
It is very hot for such music.
Gulls mistake it for a breeze.

Uncle is drunk at dinner.
It's a long toss from Block Island—
mackerel-soaked and bloodbrown,
he whistles something old,
looks at Lisa. *Did ya play today?*
A little, she answers. *It's so hot.*

Had a monster on, he says. *Big mako.*
And I lost it. Straightened the hook
right at the boat.

The question mark pulled open finally.
Did ya play? Play, dammit!
I rattle up the dishes and return
through music and cloud—
a bird's loud warning or currents
to nudge the old fish
swimming through her brain,
just after dinner, just after rain,
when our uncle's eyes thin and redden.
But my sister turns everything back. Uncle
slumps in the fighting chair.
The line goes slack.

Digging Up The Old Signal Line

A young woman with a green purse
walks toward me. She combs hair with fingers
and leaps tracks like one
who's not slept, but burned on
after a party, after sex.

> From the rusty cemetery of trains
> I watch, shovel still cold
> as six a.m. turns over
> dead line number two:
> the 6:05 arching its steam brow
> where a thick grocer in a new, black, '48 Ford waits
> for Rosedale peaches. Behind station glass,
> a woman's face. She mouths a word, raises two fingers,
> and smiles. He brings the fruit
> but bites one himself.
> Their shoulders bounce
> in laughter.

She veers toward sulking taxis.
Her chest lifts the palms
of a wilting brown dress, her green purse swings.
And in one look she smiles. Each spike rises
with the rail, the signal wires burn roots
across my hands. I hear a whistle, and remember
the station windows were nailed shut
by someone recently dead.

CASSANDRA

Who ever sees such things, Cassy?
An open crescent in the ice-packed river
where something rises to breathe. Our breath,
heavy, as we walk the unplowed span into the blue
snowbound glow of town
up the hill to Alabama Street. Billie Holiday,
wine, the stars falling
in the warm bedroom we've borrowed.

From the length of your body
I could chart that river,
melting states south
to an unmarried town of blooming lotus.
Or did you see something
that cannot be said?
Under a sheet of red, the morning sky,
our last channeled moans.
If I could only see our future, you whisper,
closing your eyes—
slivers of river
undarkened.

IV

Away

At Dawn In Beijing

A dirty glass dawn,
balconies full of bottles, mops,
busted fans and torn shirts.
Just throw that shit out, I think
for a second, lighting a cigarette.

Someone is playing a flute—really—
and that changes things. A silver reveille
for this stacked gray army.

Fluorescent light
beams across a kitchen and a woman
with long black hair and a carelessly open robe
brushes her teeth. *Maybe she's got some decent teeth*, I think,
cracking a blue duck egg on the counter.

There are noises coming on—truck engines, hammering,
yelling, a taxi driver leaning on his horn for 30 seconds.
The flute is gone. And this is a little sad.
Nothing will change.
The armies die for an ugly world.

Waiting Through Summer

Birds
freshly painted on a park bench
half-dried in the shadow
of the Forbidden City wall.
To be ancient seems so hopeless. A vast army
has been trucked in to plant trees
along the moat. Lunching on steamed bread
and soup, they politely watch willowy women
that might be wives

in another light. At the ancient observatory
I remember everything I wanted to be,
an inventor, so advanced at age ten
my work is already forgotten.
Welded into position, the armillary sphere
marks four students talking
in the park, and more soldiers
planting trees along the highway,
directing

hidden slogans in horse
drawn traffic. A greasy fax
in a dark room, whispers. More soldiers arrive
everywhere. How a country fills its time
with fear to save itself.

BLACKOUT

Bicycles speed
invisibly toward open manholes,
and from grim tanks carp leap thinking *this*
their chance. Dissolved fruit carts
and magazine stalls—
an old man stiff
in his television chair, and a woman
still clicking her abacus of lost numbers. Millions
without power and *yet*
they don't wreck the place. The screams
are children sprung
from a night school. Instant tag, laughter and
yes, tearing down a poster. *Yes*, tipping a line of bikes,
stealing a hat from a boy who's fallen—
but this is play.
Absorbed into the dusty black streets
and windowless blocks
their candle laughing
sleeps with us.
Until that bathroom light
in the middle of the night.
The freezer starting with a shiver.

New Year's At Bei Dai He, North China

There are always soldiers
and old people who stare. And some who say,
Who is he? How much does he pay?
Dusky squid light in the tide market,
opalescent rings. They see my hands like
starfish on your white thighs—a monster with money.

But we're just in love,
washing down clams and boiled cod with a bottle
of *baijiu*, hard sorghum spirits. *They sure laugh a lot,*
the waitress tells the cook
as she opens the door to a frozen night of stars.

From dark army mansions
German shepherds bark at our *Auld Lang Syne*
in English and Chinese,
and we stare at glowing, sea-crazed rocks,
and again, those stars—
you have to believe this—heavens
packed with light over a dark sea.

In the small fallen hotel
where they let us bed together
for a little extra, you light candles planted
in wobbly shells and pour tea.
I lay out blankets and put music
through our speakered walkman. The bed drifts
out to sea

where
in this sealed cabin
we are unstoppable lovers,
finding no reason to pause for the new year.
A faraway bell buoy is locked in ice,
and still it rings.

The Wall

for Jin Lei

Stretching miles beyond Monday,
we climb a windy watchtower, your hair banners
an iron sky, shaking crows and a lone farmer
from his cabbages.

Down from a mossy crenel,
you play the mortared spine's
slate melodies to an arched window
framing a river. And below, bones
on a cloudy afternoon

of brittle masons, soldiers and their starved boys
sung through with arrows. Bones or no bones,
you pick the rubble
and conjure shard, a broken dish.
Piece of nothing, I say with a toss.

Distant braying of donkeys,
that farmer loading his cart with bricks
as the sun sets his village aflicker.
Touching my cold face, frowning,
you tell me, *He's stealing the wall*.

But we're hungry. Radio music, girls skipping rope,
women frying over red-coals framed
in familiar brick. And when I turn
there's a whole dining hall that was the wall,
remortared into a welcome

that goes down easy—
rice and cabbage with bottled beer. Dark men chip
smiles across a bright table.
Laughter, pointing, and some drunk farmer
failing in his reach to offer you more,
drops a blue plate
that just won't break.

GOLDFISH

Jin Lei always dreams in bed
without me. A chalky geography
of suns. Her tea-stained teacher
taking shape without her husband's head—
toppled off somewhere south
of Suzhou.

No one is where she rises,
the old woman's soft humidity of peace—
her tea, prayers, a long gaze
on a single goldfish
suspending undulant fire.

What turns the water green?
Lei asks in a dream. Sunny Nanjing's
vegetable profusion—cucumber, cabbage,
peppers, and cress. A donkey sniffing
some woman's dress. My reach for a carp
still flapping inside a wet bag,
sticking coal dust
to a Saturday afternoon.

At the party,
students give her a photo album,
crowding out the whispers: *Why didn't she remarry?*
Her son's gone. She's getting so old!
Only a fish, one fish? Heads shake
as something hits the oil.

But this teacher
looks to the green crystal
where the blood-lit
goldfish scales its own splendor.
The scarless flanks and gauzy fantail,
the unharrassed space
of loneliness.

THE FRAGMENTARY MEMORY OF SCALES

off Teradomari, Japan

Watch the old sea,
Nihon-kai. This captain
sees nothing past his son.
And the radar smears
a very black
that's neither sky nor water
until we anchor and ignite

our ring of light. In the green
they arrive as hunters,
the *aji* and torpedo mackerel,
keeping their heads to the end.
Whole schools fooled—
our plastic jigs the dumbest prey
they've known. And before midnight,
before the last bell, the captain's boy
snags one in the black spot
behind the gill. Smiling,
showing me his luck

that's neither heads nor tails.
Drying on the rim of the blue bucket,
the fragmentary memory
of scales.

Eating Whale

Whale, there it was
right in the supermarket,
so I make a soup. To taste crime
is to believe in yourself.

I close my eyes like God,
thinking arms gone to flukes,
my fabulous tail. Seagrass, turtles,
steely blue fish—
all this
and the fatty sound
between my teeth
crackling like a thousand bubbles.

THE DEER'S VOICE

Children learn a tanka
where a deer cries autumn.
From warm futons they listen.
The 5:11 shakes their father from sleep,
grunting, sparking the old heater

and a vision that is only sound.
A poem I cannot read, but hear
sung in this apartment, far from any twig of woods,
without a park even—just a line
of twisted pine behind concrete and rail.

Hoof clicks on the road are stones,
and the snap of a willow branch
is a drunk taking a piss.
The new canals dug from the factory
sluice arrowheads. Small, taut hunters
hugged the marsh at dusk
for thirsty deer nosing through rushes. Morning is Tokyo,
Ota, Toyoda City—
uniformed workers dance
in robotic sparks along the new chassis.
And the progeny of that fossil doe
cannot really sing. They nudge children
for crackers at Nara.

The deer's cry we can hear,
this mother tells me straight. *It's my lonely heart.*
The tanka is sung again this morning,
and she smiles at her children—five and seven—
drawing amazing deer
in correct proportions. Gray crayoned
flanks and snowy tails, legs in sweet cadence.
Her husband leaves without a kiss. Wind rattles
plastic walls. I say nothing, she says nothing.
The children draw and laugh.

This Woman

Bali Island, Indonesia

Ordering delicately,
she holds the waiter seconds between—*a daiquiri, small salad,
the gado-gado, please.* A ring of light
around her wrist where a watch was. Legs
dark and bare to the sandals
stained from the sea
she might have teased. I like her. A brilliant sky
reminds me I can. She lays out postcards—the beach,
a red coral reef, the terraced rice fields
planted by straw-hatted women without shoes. Each friend
rated by the image, then the words.
For herself, she smiles,
pen between her lips, writing again
to such distance. *Excuse me*, I want to say.
Could I sit down?
But my fourth drink comes too late,
and the watch peddlers
screen me off for the wrong minutes.
She has eaten, gone,
the sun almost too low
to ever care again.

TRANCE

1.

She was one
bitter Balinese. Kicked out of heaven
for screwing the wrong god. Hair turned straw,
breasts and arms drawn down
by gravity's jungle. That angry Rangda—
her greasy spell
smeared the village gates.
She rolled in their rice, shit their wells,
and let the bravest men
fuck her from behind.

2.

After breakfast in Kuta,
I cross Bemo Corner between two vans
and a gas truck. *Eh boss, transportation?*
Watch? Ring? I give you good price. Incense smolders
in pissed-out alleys,
a dribbling horse dozes behind blinders,
and the Bali dream smells
like a wet dog chasing a chicken.

3.

Starved joy. Revenge.
Rangda's lumpy, twisted grin
churned laughter from pretty, naked girls
puking through their legs, men pissing fire
against stone. She straddled a knotted trunk
grinding to the music
of suffering.

58

4.

The volcanic spine
shadows ocean road,
and old arms swept out in black decay
sprout rice between spring veins.
Gorgeous, I say. And my driver smiles.
Bent women tread
a staggered line across terraced paddies
and a small man drives an ox.
An ox. I snap a photo, blurred by speedoed
bikers edging the road.

5.

In the attic
of a burnt-out temple
Rangda rested. Sweat dried on her woolen back
and she ate another banana slowly. Punishment maims,
revenge restores. The mangroves seethe
in wet strumming. Fiddler crab and toad,
a beetle crackling in a stork's bill,
and a young boar rooting
beneath red hibiscus. There is the far off
chant of monkeys and Brahman priests
gathering to paint the magic
masks.

6.

Where I dive
the angel fish mimics
metaphor, squeezed between nitrogen
in deep-drawn breaths sounding
relic shadows. The '42 Liberty's encrusted
bow still noses the current. And the Japs—
richer and kinder—have come back for a look. Sponges,
gorgonians, red reef coral.
A lion fish

suspends his venom dream in a rusty
cave where the torpedo may have hit.

7.

All good evil must come to an end,
an old, articulate man chuckles with the legends
on the floating pavilion.
Barong, this lion-priest here, gets his men together.
They surround Rangda and lunge
to slash her face, but her magic
turns them back. The men stab themselves
in confused frenzy.

8.

Having seen the wreck, the ray's electric carpet
and the barracuda's sidelong sneer,
I follow my smallest bubbles
to the cellophane light. Inflated,
bobbing brightly, my buddy pulls off his mask
and red crescents scar his dark cheeks.
We eat ham sandwiches on the beach. He tells me a joke
about six Japanese and an alarm clock. There's bamboo music,
a loose pig uprooting my tank,
laughter.

9.

Barong is a man of God,
and his own knife won't cut him,
the old guy tells me
as I wake on the beach
stiff and burned. *It's a man's trance,*
the knives won't go in. I hear the processional drums.
A dance—that's all it is. Rangda and Barong
parading in long costume and mask.
But these dancers look psyched to kill that witch.
Will this revenge spare women the ugliness

of sin? Spare men their humiliation?
Can these costumed boys, taller and poorer,
conjure that trance again
or will those knives
return
to the fire?

10.

I walk the cool shadow above the beach.
Parrots pivot on berried branches
and a monkey stares at me
from the crotch of a tree.

Birch Hilton

Walking late in Niigata,
a nasty wind
wings my good cap into the paddy.
So I jump the canal,
squish from clump to bristly clump,
grab the hat and see my friend Birch Hilton
and me one October years ago, boot-splitting corn stumps
in South Dakota. The fields were soaked then too,
and the pheasants wouldn't go near 'em,
so we lit a joint, and our guns grew light as brooms,
sweeping the gravel road back
to his father's house. The old man was six feet
of sleeping flannel. *Never had a New Yorker here*,
Birch whispered. We sat
at the kitchen table with a couple Old Mils
and some funky amber jello
full of fossilized fruit. His heavy lips
shaped every beer-loose story, and I laughed
'till the moment of sleep.
In that morning mirror I never saw
what stirs now in the rice-combed water.
We're jigging with the moon
leading oceans to port,
and loneliness no longer my own,
but Birch's too, for who else
ever met him like this?

V

Frozen Aperture

ON A PAINTING BY WANG MU

Blowing smoke across a scroll by Wang Mu,
boat scrubber met on the Yangtze River,
I create a possible disaster.
He tried to sell me jewelry
and I bought him a beer.
He showed me a bear claw
with a deep, blood groove. I showed him *Hustler*
and watched his black eyes burn.

Wang Mu painted this scene right
in the bar—rice paper anchored with bottles,
seconds of cliff, gorgeous gorges,
and a little drunk boatman
nearly keeling on the signature waves
of his smile.

He gave me this scroll,
but stole my wallet and watch
the next day. *The river will flow for you*, Wang Mu said,
and I believed the little shit
and still like this yellowed painting—
boatman imperiled by fog,
but alive in my room, like no other
needy artist I've known.

Frozen Aperture

Northern Ardennes, December, 1944.
The Volkswagen idles
at the sign post. *Malmedy 13 km.*
Colonel Peiper unfolds his map,
compares. His hand floats
a cloud over Belgium.
The driver is a boy, face mooning
smooth beneath the leather cap.
Hands on the wheel,
his black eyes won't drop
from the arrowed signs, crusted white
like his father's arms
parting sleet at Helmstedter Station.
He remembers a Sunday home,
pressed in dark uniform
before the parlor's drapes,
the family applause.

I smile at him
in this photograph
at the American Legion
as my uncle bends for a beer. Men shuffle
in suspenders and spangled hats—necks folded
from the long pave of Route 112, fixing TVs,
drilling teeth for thirty years.
While the boy just gazes back
into the miracle of faith,
his pulse hollow
inside an SS watch Peiper lent him
for luck in the last hours. Flak
drifting high in the gravity of dream.
My uncle wears that watch,
its crystal beaming across that German winter
where the earth blows white.
Snow? Or did some angel
flash the ground
in his sudden shutter?

THE DARWINS LOVE TO PLAY BACKGAMMON

After peeled barnacles,
cabbage seeds, quail feet
caked in mud,
teeth of rabbit and fox,
lizard eggs floating in sea water,
he plays backgammon with Emma.

They play after dinner
in the dim sitting room,
oil burned air moving
shadows over heavy chairs.
Emma throws the bones,
moves the stones,
rolls and throws again.
His eyes follow her hand to the points,
he holds the dice,
smiling past a headache.

The sparrows of Kent settle in dull trees.
England flickers yellow and blue,
Europe darkens the Atlantic.

Under June's corona
Emma pulls a blanket
over her son's tiny shoulders.
Charles lays out
yellow notes
like cards on his desk.
There's a white moth gambling
against the window.

Once There Were Great Birds In The World

1.

The bowhead whale's
scoop jaw
sweeps krill
below an Icelandic tide of great auks.
In late spring each pair steps from the upturned sea
and fumbles over the sweating rock
to lay a single egg.
When the surf is tongue-soft, thick with fish,
they lead their young back.
Black necks curl and jet
for silver—
moon-spotted crest, ax bill.

2.

When Spanish fishermen
headed northwest for cod, they would stand
and point at the rafts of great auks.
Oarsmen in red wool coats couldn't catch them,
boys couldn't hold their breath and wait.
But on the blue, white-flaked islands,
the wire-bearded men
walked among the tilted birds
and clubbed them into baskets.
At night, on ship,
they salted the garefowl, wrapping it in canvas,
and cut strips of fat into cups
to firelight their cabin faces
while the seal-wind blew.

3.

In the Iceland Natural History Museum
there's an inflated skin of a great auk.
A collector paid three fishermen,
sailing them into
the June shadows of Eldey Island
where the last pair leaned over a pointed egg,
their necks signaling alarm. And when it was over,
sheltered in the home-turned bow,
a man lit his pipe
and stroked
the bird's warm nape,
the quiet cells of the planet.

JOE LOUIS

Inside a medicine ball
he dreams a white man's waxy arm.
Thunder ring of body hooks,
the deadly right, the bloody nose
pasted up. Billy Conn's pale eyes
burning a furious thirst.

But Louis wakes in heaven,
reads another paper with his juice.
I would've beat him, said Conn.
But I tried to knock 'im out.
And a family that didn't like blacks
stood for the count.

Camp Upton on its feet
when Louis limos in. Basic training
and exhibitions. The dead-bound soldiers
cheering a fight
they'd gladly suffer.
Even the white guys wish
to be Joe Louis, God's strong side,
or the left side

where Louis stretches
from Lena Horne's bed. The war gone,
Broadway's new Buicks,
and red-gloved boxers pounding
their bruised names in leather. Hundreds
dance the ring between his ribs.

Louis drops
to his underwear,
aches into trousers, a wrinkled shirt.
The door never shuts

in this Pittsburgh wind, Billy Conn tilts
to a barking hound, rubs his face. The morning rings,
retreats in clouds, thunder, rain.
1941 again.

TALKING TO THE TORTOISE

He's talking to the tortoise.
The leather boulder blinks
out a century. But this man is Japanese,
kneeling like a boy, and he sounds serious,
struggling with all the English he's got.
Something about the tortoise's family,
or his family, or a farm lease, or furniture,
or something. Claws scratch the packed mud, the high
back is a mountain town falling
on bound bamboo and a couple
dying Toyotas. The ducks and chickens
long eaten—room for cabbage, rice.

Ah, but that's just me
drowning happiness on a sunny day,
staring over the red wall of the tortoise yard.
This man might be asking some silly shit
about ninjas or lottery numbers.
He might be drunk.
And these beasts keep to themselves, holding shells
for dear life.
The guy's trying like hell. Each syllable
for one that's lived so long
it must know something. The head turns.
Movement is a plan.

A FATHER SHOT

On a rail siding, men in yellow box cars
mix bourbon in coffee cups, play cards 'til four.
Grain rolls down from Fargo, and the whores walk home
along the tracks.

Early July sixteenth, I saw the small crowd,
and the body still in Silt Creek.
A brown hump with a tan, dry spot on top.
It's Davis, the name passed up the bank.
The sheriff stepped from his radio car.
Damn trainmen, he said. Davis' daughter
was maybe a year older. I looked into her eyes
and said *I'm really sorry.*
It wasn't for the loss, but for humiliation—
father shot holding cards and Beam.
She covered her swollen face. From then on,
I cared only for the living, begging
the dead to leave with grace.

Hotel Dreaming In Wall, South Dakota

1.

Plaster and plastic. Little white-shirted, blue-skirted pioneers bent in frantic defense, and the painted Sioux galloping down the hill's dusty shoulder.

We were large, staring into the diorama. Then we were in it, beside the wagons. Someone palmed my back—*Let's go*. We ran. *Arrows*, I thought. Wind brushed the cracked earth. Heat, heat. My collar flapped liked a grouse wing. Indians stretched bow strings across shrill throats.

Bugling. Over a tan hill sketched with scrawny bushes and rocks, the calvary charged in blue lines. Trusting the army, I made them greater—line after line. They were federal, organized, powerful. They fired rifles at the glistening brown flesh. The Indians dropped like minutes. So I made them greater. They were gutsy, unpaid, inspired. Their arrows stuck pillowy stomachs, hats flew off, tomahawks cracked fear.

Even with great control, it was still a game of hit and miss, crossfire and luck. The pioneers disappeared. The battle was grand, smoky, painted in oil. Horses reared up in gallant fury. I hummed in my own soundtrack.

2.

Some woman led me to a rocky mount. The stone was smooth, sheened like blue ore. Below the peak, an adamant face tensed at our approach. It had no eyes. The woman gestured for me to touch, but it grimaced horribly. I wasn't scared. Confidence surprised me. My fingers grazed its chin. The face twisted away, and a huge toothless mouth opened and closed slowly. I stroked its cool cheek and, finally, pressed one finger gently to its lips. It eased, but never smiled.

3.

So get your head outta da' rock, the bartender said, and the whole place laughed. Was this a joke sent as a dream? But I was still in it, and woke again in bed, thinking first of the stone, then the Indian war. I sat up, felt the table for my glasses, and heard the rain.

ON AUDUBON'S *PASSENGER PIGEON*

Heidi cradles a blue bowl, spills
tomato soup on my hand. I shake it off
and her hair sweeps down even blacker.
She's patting, laughing, wetting her lips
under warm kitchen light. The vines turn
outside glass so old it's settling soft
at the base of each lattice rib.

I think of hunting September,
staring into maples for the fragile doves
collecting by water, by night. Or walking
into the Bronx Aviary, with Heidi
pointing behind a fiberglass tree at some blazing finch
near heaven. Or meeting children on our frozen lawn
at dusk, somebody missing. A girl
picks up a dead sparrow by the wing tip
and drops it on her shoe.

This painting is before memory.
A vision of what's vanished. Its color,
some absolute blue, mortal red,
bone white long in the sharp tail.
The female twists down from a dead black gum
to feed her mate—a motion before sex.
His arched wings hold the absent sky.
No background. It is resolute,
confident, permanently mine.